Poems: A New Selection

Poems: A New Selection

Ezra Pound

Waking Lion Press

The views expressed in this book are the responsibility of the author and do not necessarily represent the position of the publisher. The reader alone is responsible for the use of any ideas or information provided by this book.

ISBN 978-1-4341-0171-6

Published by Waking Lion Press, an imprint of The Editorium

The Editorium, LLC
West Valley City, UT 84128-3917
wakinglionpress.com
wakinglion@editorium.com

Contents

From *A Lume Spento*

Grace Before Song

Lord God of heaven that with mercy dight
Th' alternate prayer wheel of the night and light
Eternal hath to thee, and in whose sight
Our days as rain drops in the sea surge fall,

As bright white drops upon a leaden sea
Grant so my songs to this grey folk may be:

As drops that dream and gleam and falling catch the sun
Evan'scent mirrors every opal one
Of such his splendor as their compass is,
So, bold My Songs, seek ye such death as this.

La Fraisne

(Scene: The Ash Wood of Malvern)

For I was a gaunt, grave councilor
Being in all things wise, and very old,
But I have put aside this folly and the cold
That old age weareth for a cloak.

I was quite strong—at least they said so—
The young men at the sword-play;
But I have put aside this folly, being gay
In another fashion that more suiteth me.

I have curled mid the boles of the ash wood,
I have hidden my face where the oak
Spread his leaves over me, and the yoke
Of the old ways of men have I cast aside.

By the still pool of Mar-nan-otha
Have I found me a bride
That was a dog-wood tree some syne.
She hath called me from mine old ways
She hath hushed my rancour of council,
Bidding me praise

Naught but the wind that flutters in the leaves.

She hath drawn me from mine old ways,
Till men say that I am mad;
But I have seen the sorrow of men, and am glad,
For I know that the wailing and bitterness are a folly.

And I? I have put aside all folly and all grief.
I wrapped my tears in an ellum leaf
And left them under a stone
And now men call me mad because I have thrown
All folly from me, putting it aside
To leave the old barren ways of men,
Because my bride
Is a pool of the wood and
Tho all men say that I am mad
It is only that I am glad,
Very glad, for my bride hath toward me a great love
That is sweeter than the love of women
That plague and burn and drive one away.

Aie-e! 'Tis true that I am gay
        Quite gay, for I have her alone here
        And no man troubleth us.

Once when I was among the young men . . . .
And they said I was quite strong, among the young
Once there was a woman . . . .
. . . . but I forget . . . . she was . . . .
. . . . I hope she will not come again.

. . . . I do not remember . . . .
I think she hurt me once but . . . .
That was very long ago.

I do not like to remember things any more.

I like one little band of winds that blow
In the ash trees here:
For we are quite alone
Here mid the ash trees.

Cino

(Italian Campagna 1309, the open road)

Bah! I have sung women in three cities,
But it is all the same;
And I will sing of the sun.

Lips, words, and you snare them,
Dreams, words, and they are as jewels,
Strange spells of old deity,
Ravens, nights, allurement:
And they are not;
Having become the souls of song.

Eyes, dreams, lips, and the night goes.
Being upon the road once more,
They are not.
Forgetful in their towers of our tuneing
Once for wind-runeing
They dream us-toward and
Sighing, say, "Would Cino,
Passionate Cino, of the wrinkling eyes,
Gay Cino, of quick laughter,
Cino, of the dare, the jibe.
Frail Cino, strongest of his tribe
That tramp old ways beneath the sun-light,
Would Cino of the Luth were here!"

Once, twice a year—
Vaguely thus word they:
    "Cino?" "Oh, eh, Cino Polnesi
    The singer is't you mean?"
    "Ah yes, passed once our way,
    A saucy fellow, but . . .
    (Oh they are all one these vagabonds),
    Peste! 'tis his own songs?
    Or some other's that he sings?
    But *you*, My Lord, how with your city?"

But you "My Lord," God's pity!
And all I knew were out, My Lord, you
Were Lack-land Cino, e'en as I am,
O Sinistro.

I have sung women in three cities.
But it is all one.
I will sing of the sun.
. . . . eh? . . . . they mostly had grey eyes,
But it is all one, I will sing of the sun.

        "'Pollo Phoibee, old tin pan, you
        Glory to Zeus' aegis-day,
        Shield o' steel-blue, th' heaven o'er us
        Hath for boss thy lustre gay!

        'Pollo Phoibee, to our way-fare
        Make thy laugh our wander-lied;
        Bid thy 'flugence bear away care.
        Cloud and rain-tears pass they fleet!

        Seeking e'er the new-laid rast-way
        To the gardens of the sun . . .

                    * * *

7

I have sung women in three cities
But it is all one.

I will sing of the white birds
In the blue waters of heaven,
The clouds that are spray to its sea."

In Epitaphium Eius

Servant and singer, Troubador
That for his loving, loved each fair face more
Than craven sluggard can his life's one love,

Dowered with love, "whereby the sun doth move
And all the stars."
They called him fickle that the lambent flame
Caught "Bicé" dreaming in each new-blown name,

And loved all fairness tho its hidden guise
Lurked various in half an hundred eyes;

That loved the essence tho each casement bore
A different semblance than the one before.

Villonaud for This Yule

Towards the Noel that morte saison
(Christ make the shepherds' homage dear!)
Then when the grey wolves everychone
Drink of the winds their chill small-beer
And lap o' the snows food's gueredon
Then makyth my heart his yule-tide cheer
(Skoal! with the dregs if the clear be gone!)
Wineing the ghosts of yester-year.

Ask ye what ghost I dream upon?
(What of the magians' scented gear?)
The ghosts of dead loves everyone
That make the stark winds reek with fear
Lest love return with the foison sun
And slay the memories that me cheer
(Such as I drink to mine fashion)
Wineing the ghosts of yester-year.

Where are the joys my heart had won?
(Saturn and Mars to Zeus drawn near!)
Where are athe lips mine lay upon,
Aye! where are the glances feat and clear
That bade my heart his valor don?

I skoal to the eyes as grey-blown meer
(Who knows whose was that paragon?)
Wineing the ghosts of yester-year.

Prince: ask me not what I have done
Nor what God hath that can me cheer
But ye ask first where the winds are gone
Wineing the ghosts of yester-year.

Masks

These tales of old disguisings, are they not
Strange myths of souls that found themselves among
Unwonted folk that spake an hostile tongue,
Some soul from all the rest who'd not forgot
The star-span acres of a former lot
Where boundless mid the clouds his course he swung,
Or carnate with his elder brothers sung
Ere ballad-makers lisped of Camelot?

Old singers half-forgetful of their tunes,
Old painters color-blind come back once more,
Old poets skill-less in the wind-heart runes,
Old wizards lacking in their wonder-lore:

All they that with strange sadness in their eyes
Ponder in silence o'er earth's queynt devyse?

Invern

Earth's winter cometh
And I being part of all
And sith the spirit of all moveth in me
I must needs bear earth's winter
Drawn cold and grey with hours
And joying in a momentary sun,
Lo I am withered with waiting till my spring cometh!
Or crouch covetous of warmth
O'er scant-logged ingle blaze,
Must take cramped joy in tomed Longinus
That, read I him first time
The woods agleam with summer
Or mid desirous winds of spring,
Had set me singing spheres
Or made heart to wander forth among warm roses
Or curl in grass next neath a kindly moon.

Ballad for Gloom

For God, our God is a gallant foe
That playeth behind the veil.

I have loved my God as a child at heart
That seeketh deep bosoms for rest,
I have loved my God as a maid to man—
But lo, this thing is best:

To love your God as a gallant foe
                    that plays behind the veil;
To meet your God as the night winds meet
                    beyond Arcturus' pale.

I have played with God for a woman,
I have staked with my God for truth,
I have lost to my God as a man, clear-eyed—
    His dice be not of ruth.

For I am made as a naked blade,
    But hear ye this thing in sooth:

Who loseth to God as man to man
    Shall win at the turn of the game.
I have drawn my blade where the lightnings meet
    But the ending is the same:
Who loseth to God as the sword blades lose
    Shall win at the end of the game.

For God, our God, is a gallant foe
             that playeth behind the veil.
Whom God deigns not to overthrow
               Hath need of triple mail.

Prometheus

For we be the beaten wands
And the bearers of the flame.
    Our selves have died lang syne, and we
Go ever upward as the sparks of light
Enkindling all
'Gainst whom our shadows fall.

Weary to sink, yet ever upward borne,
Flame, flame that riseth ever
To the flame within the sun,
Tearing our casement ever
For the way is one
That beareth upward
To the flame within the sun.

La Regina Avrillouse

Lady of rich allure,
Queen of the spring's embrace,
Your arms are long like boughs of ash,
Mid laugh-broken streams, spirit of rain unsure,
Breath of the poppy flower,
All the wood thy bower
    And the hills thy dwelling-place.

This will I no more dream;
Warm is thy arm's allure,
Warm is the gust of breath
That ere thy lips meet mine
Kisseth my cheek and saith:
"This is the joy of earth,
Here is the wine of mirth
    Drain ye one goblet sure,

Take ye the honey cup
The honied song raise up,
Drink of the spring's allure,
April and dew and rain;
Brown of the earth sing sure,
Cheeks and lips and hair
And soft breath that kisseth where
    Thy lips have come not yet to drink."

Moss and the mold of earth,
These be thy couch of mirth,
Long arms thy boughs of shade
April-alluring, as the blade
Of grass doth catch the dew
And make it crown to hold the sun.
Banner be you
    Above my head,
Glory to all wold display'd,
    April-alluring, glory-bold.

In Tempore Senectutis

(An Anti-stave for Dowson)

When I am old
I will not have you look apart
From me, into the cold,
Friend of my heart,
Nor be sad in your remembrance
Of the careless, mad-heart semblance
That the wind hath blown away
When I am old.

When I am old
And the white hot wonder-fire
Unto the world seem cold,
My soul's desire
Know you then that all life's shower,
The rain of the years, that hour
Shall make blow for us one flower,
Including all, when we are old.

When I am old
If you remember
Any love save what is then
Hearth light unto life's December
Be your joy of past sweet chalices
To know then naught but this
"How many wonders are less sweet
Than love I bear to thee
When I am old."

Make-strong old dreams lest this our world
lose heart.

For man is a skinfull of wine
But his soul is a hole full of God
And the song of all time blows thru him
As winds through a knot-holed board.

Tho man be a skin full of wine
Yet his heart is a little child
That croucheth low beneath the wind
When the God-storm battereth wild.

From *A Quinzaine for This Yule*

Histrion

No man hath dared to write this thing as yet,
And yet I know, how that the souls of all men great
At times pass athrough us,
And we are melted into them, and are not
Save reflexions of their souls.
Thus am I Dante for a space and am
One Francois Villon, ballad-lord and thief,
Or am such holy ones I may not write
Lest blasphemy be writ against my name;
This for an instant and the flame is gone.

'Tis as in midmost us there glows a sphere
Translucent, molten gold, that is the "I"
And into this some form projects itself:
Christus, or John, or eke the Florentine;
And as the clear space is not if a form's
Imposed thereon,
So cease we from all being for the time,
And these, the Masters of the Soul, live on.

From *Personae* (1909)

Praise of Ysolt

In vain have I striven
      to teach my heart to bow;
In vain have I said to him
"There be many singers greater than thou."
But his answer cometh, as winds and as lutany,
As a vague crying upon the night
That leaveth me no rest, saying ever,
          "Song, a song."

Their echoes play upon each other in the twilight
Seeking ever a song.
Lo, I am worn with travail
And the wandering of many roads hath made my eyes
As dark red circles filled with dust.
Yet there is a trembling upon me in the twilight,
    And little red elf words   crying "A song,"
    Little grey elf words   crying for a song,
    Little brown leaf words   crying "A song,"
    Little green leaf words   crying for a song.
The words are as leaves, old brown leaves in the spring time
Blowing they know not whither, seeking a song.

White words as snow flakes but they are cold
Moss words, lip words, words of slow streams.

In vain have I striven
      to teach my soul to bow,

In vain have I pled with him,
        "There be greater souls than thou."

For in the morn of my years there came a woman
As moon light calling
As moon calleth the tides,
        "Song, a song."
Wherefore I made her a song and she went from me
As the moon doth from the sea,
But still came the leaf words, little brown elf words
Saying "The soul sendeth us."
                "A song, a song!"
And in vain I cried unto them "I have no song
For she I sang of hath gone from me."

But my soul sent a woman, a woman of the wonderfolk,
A woman as fire upon the pine woods
        crying "Song, a song."
As the flame crieth unto the sap.
My song was ablaze with her and she went from me
As flame leaveth the embers so went she unto new forests
And the words were with me
        crying ever "Song, a song."

And I "I have no song,"
Till my soul sent a woman as the sun:
Yea as the sun calleth to the seed,
As the spring upon the bough
So is she that cometh the song-drawer
She that holdeth the wonder words within her eyes
The words little elf words
        that call ever unto me
                "Song, a song."

Envoi

In vain have I striven with my soul
    to teach my soul to bow.
What soul boweth
    while in his heart art thou?

In the Old Age of the Soul

I do not choose to dream; there cometh on me
Some strange old lust for deeds.
As to the nerveless hand of some old warrior
The sword-hilt or the war-worn wonted helmet
Brings momentary life and long-fled cunning,
So to my soul grown old—
Grown old with many a jousting, many a foray,
Grown old with many a hither-coming and hence-going—
Till now they send him dreams and no more deed;
So doth he flame again with might for action,
Forgetful of the council of elders,
Forgetful that who rules doth no more battle,
Forgetful that such might no more cleaves to him
So doth he flame again toward valiant doing.

The White Stag

I ha' seen them 'mid the clouds on the heather.
Lo! they pause not for love nor for sorrow,
Yet their eyes are as the eyes of a maid to her lover,
When the white hart breaks his cover
And the white wind breaks the morn.

"'Tis the white stag, Fame, we're a-hunting,
Bid the world's hounds come to horn!"

Piccadilly

Beautiful, tragical faces—
Ye that were whole, and are so sunken;
And, O ye vile, ye that might have been loved,
That are so sodden and drunken,
      Who hath forgotten you?

O wistful, fragile faces, few out of many!

The crass, the coarse, the brazen,
God knows I cannot pity them, perhaps, as I should do;
But oh, ye delicate, wistful faces,
      Who hath forgotten you?

From *Exultations*

Ballad of the Goodly Fere[1]

Simon Zelotes speaketh it somewhile after the Crucifixion.

Ha' we lost the goodliest fere o' all
For the priests and the gallows tree?
Aye lover he was of brawny men,
O' ships and the open sea.

When they came wi' a host to take Our Man
His smile was good to see,
"First let these go!" quo' our Goodly Fere,
"Or I'll see ye damned," says he.

Aye he sent us out through the crossed high spears
And the scorn of his laugh rang free,
"Why took ye not me when I walked about
Alone in the town?" says he.

Oh we drank his "Hale" in the good red wine
When we last made company,
No capon priest was the Goodly Fere
But a man o' men was he.

I ha' seen him drive a hundred men
Wi' a bundle o' cords swung free,

---

1. Fere = Mate, Companion.

That they took the high and holy house
For their pawn and treasury.

They'll no' get him a' in a book I think
Though they write it cunningly;
No mouse of the scrolls was the Goodly Fere
But aye loved the open sea.

If they think they ha' snared our Goodly Fere
They are fools to the last degree.
"I'll go to the feast," quo' our Goodly Fere,
"Though I go to the gallows tree."

"Ye ha' seen me heal the lame and blind,
And wake the dead," says he,
"Ye shall see one thing to master all:
'Tis how a brave man dies on the tree."

A son of God was the Goodly Fere
That bade us his brothers be.
I ha' seen him cow a thousand men.
I have seen him upon the tree.

He cried no cry when they drave the nails
And the blood gushed hot and free,
The hounds of the crimson sky gave tongue
But never a cry cried he.

I ha' seen him cow a thousand men
On the hills o' Galilee,
They whined as he walked out calm between,
Wi' his eyes like the grey o' the sea,

Like the sea that brooks no voyaging
With the winds unleashed and free,
Like the sea that he cowed at Genseret
Wi' twey words spoke' suddently.

A master of men was the Goodly Fere,
A mate of the wind and sea,
If they think they ha' slain our Goodly Fere
They are fools eternally.

I ha' seen him eat o' the honey-comb
Sin' they nailed him to the tree.

Francesca

You came in out of the night
And there were flowers in your hand,
Now you will come out of a confusion of people,
Out of a turmoil of speech about you.

I who have seen you amid the primal things
Was angry when they spoke your name
In ordinary places.
I would that the cool waves might flow over my mind,
And that the world should dry as a dead leaf,
Or as a dandelion see-pod and be swept away,
So that I might find you again,
Alone.

A Song of the Virgin Mother

In the play "Los Pastores de Belen"
From the Spanish of Lope de Vega

As ye go through these palm-trees
O holy angels;
Sith sleepeth my child here
Still ye the branches.

O Bethlehem palm-trees
That move to the anger
Of winds in their fury,
Tempestuous voices,
Make ye no clamour,
Run ye less swiftly,
Sith sleepeth the child here,
Still ye your branches.

He the divine child
Is here a-wearied
Of weeping the earth-pain,
Here for his rest would he
Cease from his mourning,
Only a little while
Sith sleepeth this child here,
Stay ye the branches.

Cold be the fierce winds,
Treacherous round him.
Ye see that I have not
Wherewith to guard him,
O angels, divine ones
That pass us a-flying,
Sith sleepeth my child here,
Stay ye the branches.

From *The Spirit of Romance*

A War Song

From the Provençal of Bertrand de Born
(c. 1140–1214)

Well pleaseth me the sweet time of Easter
That maketh the leaf and the flower come out.
And it pleaseth me when I hear the clamor
Of the birds, their song through the wood;
And it pleaseth me when I see through the meadows
The tents and pavilions set up, and great joy have I
When I see o'er the campagna knights armed and horses arrayed.

And it pleaseth me when the scouts set in flight the folk with their
    goods;
And it pleaseth me when I see coming together after them an host of
    armed men.
And it pleaseth me to the heart when I see strong castles beseiged,
And barriers broken and riven, and I see the host on the shore all
    about shut in with ditches,
And closed in with lisses of strong piles.

Cantico del Sole

The thought of what America would be like
If the Classics had a wide circulation
        Troubles my sleep,
The thought of what America,
The thought of what America,
The thought of what America would be like
If the Classics had a wide circulation
        Troubles my sleep.
Nunc dimittis, now lettest thou thy servant,
Now lettest thou thy servant
        Depart in peace.
The thought of what America,
The thought of what America,
The thought of what America would be like
If the Classics had a wide circulation . . .
        Oh well!
        It troubles my sleep.

From *Canzoni*

The Tree

I stood still and was a tree amid the wood,
Knowing the truth of things unseen before;
Of Daphne and the laurel bow
And that god-feasting couple old
that grew elm-oak amid the wold.
'Twas not until the gods had been
Kindly entreated, and been brought within
Unto the hearth of their heart's home
That they might do this wonder thing;
Nathless I have been a tree amid the wood
And many a new thing understood
That was rank folly to my head before.

Canzon: The Yearly Slain

(Written in reply to Manning's "Korè")

I

Ah! red-leafed time hath driven out the rose
And crimson dew is fallen on the leaf
Ere ever yet the cold white wheat be sown
That hideth all earth's green and sere and red;
The Moon-flower's fallen and the branch is bare,
Holding no honey for the starry bees;
The Maiden turns to her dark lord's demesne.

II

Fairer than Enna's field when Ceres sows
The stars of hyacinth and puts off grief,
Fairer than petals on May morning blown
Through apple-orchards where the sun hath shed
His brighter petals down to make their fair;
Fairer than these the Poppy-crowned one flees,
And Joy goes weeping in her scarlet train.

III

The faint damp wind that, ere the even, blows
Piling the west with many a tawny sheaf,
Then when the last glad wavering hours are mown
Sigheth and dies because the day is sped;
This wind is like her and the listless air
Wherewith she goeth by beneath the trees,
The trees that mock her with their scarlet stain.

IV

Love that is born of Time and comes and goes!
Love that doeth hold all noble hearts in fief!
As red leaves follow where the wind hath flown,
So all men follow Love when Love is dead.
O Fate of Wind! O Wind that cannot spare,
But drivest out the Maid, and pourest lees
Of all thy crimson on the wold again,

V

Korè my heart is, let it stand sans gloze!
Love's pain is long, and lo, love's joy is brief!
My heart erst alway sweet is bitter grown;
As crimson ruleth in the good green's stead,
So grief hath taken all mine old joy's share
And driven forth my solace and all ease
Where pleasure bows to all-usurping pain.

VI

Crimson the hearth where one last ember glows!
My heart's new winter hath no such relief,
Nor thought of Spring whose blossom he hath known
Hath turned him back where Spring is banishèd.
Barren the heart and dead the fires there,
Blow! O ye ashes, where the winds shall please,
But cry, "Love also is the Yearly Slain."

VII

Be sped, my Canzon, through the bitter air!
To him who speaketh words as fair as these,
Say that I also know the "Yearly Slain."

Ballatetta

The light became her grace and dwelt among
Blind eyes and shadows that are formed as men;
Lo, how the light doth melt us into song:

The broken sunlight for a healm she beareth
Who has my heart in jurisdiction.
In wild-wood never fawn nor fallow fareth
So silent light; no gossamer is spun
So delicate as she is, when the sun
Drives the clear emeralds from the bended grasses
Lest they should parch too swiftly, where she passes.

Prayer for His Lady's Life

From Propertius, Elegiae, *Lib. III, 26*

Here let thy clemency, Persephone, hold firm,
Do thou, Pluto, bring here no greater harshness.
So many thousand beauties are gone down to Avernus,
Ye might let one remain above with us.

With you is Iope, with you the white-gleaming Tyro,
With you is Europa and the shameless Pasiphae,
And all the fair from Troy and all from Achaia,
From the sundered realms, of Thebes and of aged Priamus;
And all the maidens of Rome, as many as they were,
They died and the greed of your flame consumes them.

Here let thy clemency, Persephone, hold firm,
Do thou, Pluto, bring here no greater harshness.
So many thousand fair are gone down to Avernus,
Ye might let one remain above with us.

Maestro di Tocar

(W.R.)

You, who are touched not by our mortal ways
Nor girded with the stricture of our bands,
Have but to loose the magic from your hands
And all men's hearts that glimmer for a day,
And all our loves that are so swift to flame
Rise in that space of sound and melt away.

Aria

My love is a deep flame
          that hides beneath the waters.

—My love is gay and kind,
My love is hard to find
      as the flame beneath the waters.

The fingers of the wind
               meet hers
With a frail
          swift greeting.
My love is gay
          and kind
               and hard
                    of meeting,
As the flame beneath the waters
               hard of meeting.

Song in the Manner of Housman

O woe, woe,
People are born and die,
We also shall be dead pretty soon
Therefore let us act as if we were
                    dead already.

The bird sits on the hawthorn tree
But he dies also, presently.
Some lads get hung, and some get shot.
Woeful is this human lot.
                    Woe! woe, etcetera. . . .

London is a woeful place,
Shropshire is much pleasanter.
Then let us smile a little space
Upon fond nature's morbid grace.
                    Oh, Woe, woe, woe, etcetera. . . .

From Translations from Heine

Von "Die Heimkehr"

Is your hate, then, of such measure?
Do you, truly, so detest me?
Through all the world will I complain
Of how you have addressed me.

O ye lips that are ungrateful,
Hath it never once distressed you,
That you can say such awful things
Of any one who ever kissed you?

From Und Drang

The House of Splendour

'Tis Evenoe's,
A house not made with hands,
But out somewhere beyond the worldly ways
Her gold is spread, above, around, inwoven
Strange ways and walls are fashioned out of it.

And I have seen my Lady in the sun,
Her hair was spread about, a sheaf of wings,
And red the sunlight was, behind it all.

And I have seen her there within her house,
With six great sapphires hung along the wall,
Low, panel-shaped, a-level with her knees,
And all her robe was woven of pale gold.

There are many rooms and all of gold,
Of woven walls deep patterned, of email,
Of beaten work; and through the claret stone,
Set to some weaving, comes the aureate light.

Here am I come perforce my love of her,
Behold mine adoration
Maketh me clear, and there are powers in this
Which, played on by the virtues of her soul,
Break down the four-square walls of standing time.

From *Ripostes*

Silet

When I behold how black, immortal ink
Drips from my deathless pen—ah, well-away!
Why should we stop at all for what I think?
. There is enough in what I chance to say.

It is enough that we once came together;
What is the use of setting it to rime?
When it is autumn do we get spring weather,
Or gather may of harsh northwindish time?

It is enough that we once came together;
What if the wind have turned against the rain?
It is enough that we once came together;
Time has seen this, and will not turn again;

And who are we, who know that last intent,
To plague to-morrow with a testament!

Portrait d'Une Femme

Your mind and you are our Sargasso Sea,
London has swept about you this score years
And bright ships left you this or that in fee:
Ideas, old gossip, oddments of all things,
Strange spars of knowledge and dimmed wares of price.
Great minds have sought you- lacking someone else.
You have been second always. Tragical?
No. You preferred it to the usual thing:
One dull man, dulling and uxorious,
One average mind- with one thought less, each year.
Oh, you are patient, I have seen you sit
Hours, where something might have floated up.
And now you pay one. Yes, you richly pay.
You are a person of some interest, one comes to you
And takes strange gain away:
Trophies fished up; some curious suggestion;
Fact that leads nowhere; and a tale for two,
Pregnant with mandrakes, or with something else
That might prove useful and yet never proves,
That never fits a corner or shows use,
Or finds its hour upon the loom of days:
The tarnished, gaudy, wonderful old work;
Idols and ambergris and rare inlays,
These are your riches, your great store; and yet
For all this sea-hoard of deciduous things,
Strange woods half sodden, and new brighter stuff:

In the slow float of differing light and deep,
No! there is nothing! In the whole and all,
Nothing that's quite your own.
                    Yet this is you.

A Girl

The tree has entered my hands,
The sap has ascended my arms,
The tree has grown in my breast—Downward,
The branches grow out of me, like arms.

Tree you are,
Moss you are,
You are violets with wind above them.
A child—*so* high—you are,
And all this is folly to the world.

Quies

This is another of our ancient loves.
Pass and be silent, Rullus, for the day
Hath lacked a something since this lady passed;
Hath lacked a something. 'Twas but marginal.

The Seafarer

(From the early Anglo-Saxon text)

May I for my own self song's truth reckon,
Journey's jargon, how I in harsh days
Hardship endured oft.
Bitter breast-cares have I abided,
Known on my keel many a care's hold,
And dire sea-surge, and there I oft spent
Narrow nightwatch nigh the ship's head
While she tossed close to cliffs. Coldly afflicted,
My feet were by frost benumbed.
Chill its chains are; chafing sighs
Hew my heart round and hunger begot
Mere-weary mood. Lest man know not
That he on dry land loveliest liveth,
List how I, care-wretched, on ice-cold sea,
Weathered the winter, wretched outcast
Deprived of my kinsmen;
Hung with hard ice-flakes, where hail-scur flew,
There I heard naught save the harsh sea
And ice-cold wave, at whiles the swan cries,
Did for my games the gannet's clamour,
Sea-fowls, loudness was for me laughter,
The mews' singing all my mead-drink.
Storms, on the stone-cliffs beaten, fell on the stern
In icy feathers; full oft the eagle screamed

With spray on his pinion.
                    Not any protector
May make merry man faring needy.
This he little believes, who aye in winsome life
Abides 'mid burghers some heavy business,
Wealthy and wine-flushed, how I weary oft
Must bide above brine.
Neareth nightshade, snoweth from north,
Frost froze the land, hail fell on earth then
Corn of the coldest. Nathless there knocketh now
The heart's thought that I on high streams
The salt-wavy tumult traverse alone.
Moaneth alway my mind's lust
That I fare forth, that I afar hence
Seek out a foreign fastness.
For this there's no mood-lofty man over earth's midst,
Not though he be given his good, but will have in his youth greed;
Nor his deed to the daring, nor his king to the faithful
But shall have his sorrow for sea-fare
Whatever his lord will.
He hath not heart for harping, nor in ring-having
Nor winsomeness to wife, nor world's delight
Nor any whit else save the wave's slash,
Yet longing comes upon him to fare forth on the water.
Bosque taketh blossom, cometh beauty of berries,
Fields to fairness, land fares brisker,
All this admonisheth man eager of mood,
The heart turns to travel so that he then thinks
On flood-ways to be far departing.
Cuckoo calleth with gloomy crying,
He singeth summerward, bodeth sorrow,
The bitter heart's blood. Burgher knows not—
He the prosperous man—what some perform
Where wandering them widest draweth.
So that but now my heart burst from my breast-lock,
My mood 'mid the mere-flood,

Over the whale's acre, would wander wide.
On earth's shelter cometh often to me,
Eager and ready, the crying lone-flyer,
Whets for the whale-path the heart irresistibly,
O'er tracks of ocean; seeing that anyhow
My lord deems to me this dead life
On loan and on land, I believe not
That any earth-weal eternal standeth
Save there be somewhat calamitous
That, ere a man's tide go, turn it to twain.
Disease or oldness or sword-hate
Beats out the breath from doom-gripped body.
And for this, every earl whatever, for those speaking after—
Laud of the living, boasteth some last word,
That he will work ere he pass onward,
Frame on the fair earth 'gainst foes his malice,
Daring ado, . . .
So that all men shall honour him after
And his laud beyond them remain 'mid the English,
Aye, for ever, a lasting life's-blast,
Delight mid the doughty.
                              Days little durable,
And all arrogance of earthen riches,
There come now no kings nor Caesars
Nor gold-giving lords like those gone.
Howe'er in mirth most magnified,
Whoe'er lived in life most lordliest,
Drear all this excellence, delights undurable!
Waneth the watch, but the world holdeth.
Tomb hideth trouble. The blade is layed low.
Earthly glory ageth and seareth.
No man at all going the earth's gait,
But age fares against him, his face paleth,
Grey-haired he groaneth, knows gone companions,
Lordly men are to earth o'ergiven,
Nor may he then the flesh-cover, whose life ceaseth,

Nor eat the sweet nor feel the sorry,
Nor stir hand nor think in mid heart,
And though he strew the grave with gold,
His born brothers, their buried bodies
Be an unlikely treasure hoard.

An Immorality

Sing we for love and idleness,
Naught else is worth the having.

Though I have been in many a land,
There is naught else in living.

And I would rather have my sweet,
Though rose-leaves die of grieving,

Than do high deeds in Hungary
To pass all men's believing.

The Needle

Come, or the stellar tide will slip away.
Eastward avoid the hour of its decline,
Now! for the needle trembles in my soul!

Here we have had our vantage, the good hour.
Here we have had our day, your day and mine.
Come now, before this power
That bears us up, shall turn against the pole.

Mock not the flood of stars, the thing's to be.
O Love, come now, this land turns evil slowly.
The waves bore in, soon they bear away.

The treasure is ours, make we fast land with it.
Move we and take the tide, with its next favour,
Abide
Under some neutral force
Until this course turneth aside.

Sub Mare

It is, and is not, I am sane enough,
Since you have come this place has hovered round me,
This fabrication built of autumn roses,
Then there's a goldish colour, different.

And one gropes in these things as delicate
Algæ reach up and out, beneath
Pale slow green surgings of the underwave,
'Mid these things older than the names they have,
These things that are familiars of the god.

Plunge

I would bathe myself in strangeness:
These comforts heaped upon me, smother me!
I burn, I scald so for the new,
New friends, new faces,
Places!
Oh to be out of this,
This that is all I wanted
        —save the new.
And you,
Love, you the much, the more desired!
Do I not loathe all walls, streets, stones,
All mire, mist, all fog,
All ways of traffic?
You, I would have flow over me like water,
Oh, but far out of this!
Grass, and low fields, and hills,
And sun,
Oh, sun enough!
Out, and alone, among some
Alien people!

The Return

See, they return; ah, see the tentative
    Movements, and the slow feet,
    The trouble in the pace and the uncertain
    Wavering!

See, they return, one, and by one,
With fear, as half-awakened;
As if the snow should hesitate
And murmur in the wind,
             and half turn back;
These were the "Wing'd-with-Awe,"
        Inviolable.

Gods of the wingèd shoe!
With them the silver hounds,
        sniffing the trace of air!

Haie! Haie!
    These were the swift to harry;
    These the keen-scented;
    These were the souls of blood.

Slow on the leash,
             pallid the leash-men!

From *Cathay*

Translations by Ezra Pound

For the most part from the Chinese of
Rihaku, from the notes of the
late Ernest Fenollosa, and
the decipherings of the
professors Mori
and Ariga

Song of the Bowman of Shu

Here we are, picking the first fern-shoots
And saying: When shall we get back to our country?
Here we are because we have the Ken-nin for our foemen,
We have no comfort because of these Mongols.
We grub the soft fern-shoots,
When anyone says "Return," the others are full of sorrow.
Sorrowful minds, sorrow is strong, we are hungry and thirsty.
Our defence is not yet made sure, no one can let his friend return.
We grub the old fern-stalks.
We say: Will we be let to go back in October?
There is no ease in royal affairs, we have no comfort.
Our sorrow is bitter, but we would not return to our country.
What flower has come into blossom?
Whose chariot? The General's.
Horses, his horses even, are tired. They were strong.
We have no rest, three battles a month.
By heaven, his horses are tired.
The generals are on them, the soldiers are by them.
The horses are well trained, the generals have ivory arrows and
quivers ornamented with fish-skin.
The enemy is swift, we must be careful.
When we set out, the willows were drooping with spring,
We come back in the snow,
We go slowly, we are hungry and thirsty,
Our mind is full of sorrow, who will know of our grief?

By Kutsugen.
4th Century B.C.

The Beautiful Toilet

Blue, blue is the grass about the river
And the willows have overfilled the close garden.
And within, the mistress, in the midmost of her youth,
White, white of face, hesitates, passing the door.
Slender. she puts forth a slender hand;

And she was a courtezan in the old days,
And she has married a sot,
Who now goes drunkenly out
And leaves her too much alone.

By Mei Sheng.
B.C. 140

The River Song

This boat is of shato-wood, and its gunwales are cut magnolia,
Musicians with jeweled flutes and with pipes of gold
Fill full the sides in rows, and our wine
Is rich for a thousand cups.
We carry singing girls, drift with the drifting water,
Yet Sennin needs
A yellow stork for a charger, and all our seamen
Would follow the white gulls or ride them.
Kutsu's prose song
Hangs with the sun and moon.

King So's terraced palace
                    is now but barren hill,
But I draw pen on this barge
Causing the five peaks to tremble,
And I have joy in these words
                    like the joy of blue islands.
(If glory could last forever
Then the waters of Han would flow northward.)

And I have moped in the Emperor's garden, awaiting an
    order-to-write!
I looked at the dragon-pond, with its willow-colored water
Just reflecting in the sky's tinge,
And heard the five-score nightingales aimlessly singing.

The eastern wind brings the green color into the island grasses at
    Yei-shu,
The purple house and the crimson are full of Spring softness.
South of the pond the willow-tips are half-blue and bluer,
Their cords tangle in mist, against the brocade-like palace.
Vine strings a hundred feet long hang down from carved railings,
And high over the willows, the find birds sing to each other, and
    listen,
Crying—'Kwan, Kuan,' for the early wind, and the feel of it.
The wind bundles itself into a bluish cloud and wanders off.
Over a thousand gates. over a thousand doors are the sounds of
[Warning: Image not found] spring singing,
And the Emperor is at Ko.
Five clouds hang aloft, bright on the purple sky,
The imperial guards come forth from the goldren house with their
[Warning: Image not found] armor a-gleaming.
The Emperor in his jeweled car goes out to inspect his flowers,
He goes out to Hori, to look at the wing-flapping storks,
He returns by way of Sei rock, to hear the new nightingales,
For the gardens of Jo-run are full of new nightingales,
Their sound is mixed in this flute,
Their voice is in the twelve pipes here.

By Rihaku.
8th Century A.D.

The River Merchant's Wife: A Letter

While my hair was still cut straight across my forehead
Played I about the front gate, pulling flowers.
You came by on bamboo stilts, playing horse,
You walked about my seat, playing with blue plums.
And we went on living in the village of Chokan:
Two small people, without dislike or suspicion.

At fourteen I married My Lord you,
I never laughed, being bashful.
Lowering my head, I looked at the wall.
Called to, a thousand times, I never looked back.

At fifteen I stopped scowling,
I desired my dust to be mingled with yours
Forever and forever and forever.
Why should I climb the look out?

At sixteen you departed,
You went into fat Ku-to-yen, by the river of swirling eddies,
And you have been gone five months.
The monkeys make sorrowful noise overhead.
You dragged your feet when you went out.
By the gate now, the moss is grown, the different mosses,
Too deep to clear them away!
The leaves fall early in autumn, in wind.
The paired butterflies are already yellow with August
Over the grass in the West garden;

They hurt me.
I grow older.
If you are coming down through the narrows of the river Kiang,
Please let me know beforehand,
And I will come out to meet you
                    As far as Cho-fu-Sa.

                                        By Rihaku.

The Jewel Stair's Grievance[1]

The jewelled steps are already quite white with dew,
It is so late the dew soaks my gauze stockings,
And I let down the crystal curtain
And watch the moon through the clear autumn.

By Rihaku.

---

1. Jewel stairs, therefore a palace. Grievance, therefore there is something to complain of. Gauze stockings, therefore a court lady, not a servant who complains. Clear autumn, there fore he has no excuse on account of the weather. Also she has come early, for the dew has not merely whitened the stairs, but soaks her stockings. The poem is especially prized because she utters no direct reproach.

Poem by the Bridge at Ten-Shin

March has come to the bridge head,
Peach boughs and apricot boughs hang over a thousand gates,
At morning there are flowers to cut the heart,
And evening drives them on the eastward-flowing waters.
Petals are on the gone waters and on the going,
    And on the back-swirling eddies,
But to-day's men are not the men of the old days,
Though they hang in the same way over the bridge-rail.

The sea's colour moves at the dawn
And the princes still stand in rows, about the throne,
And the moon falls over the portals of Sei-go-yo,
And clings to the walls and the gate-top.
With head-gear glittering against the cloud and sun,
The lords go forth from the court, and into far borders.
They ride upon dragon-like horses,
Upon horses with head-trappings of yellow-metal,
And the streets make way for their passage.
             Haughty their passing,
Haughty their steps as they go into great banquets,
To high halls and curious food,
To the perfumed air and girls dancing,
To clear flutes and clear singing;
To the dance of the seventy couples;
To the mad chase through the gardens.
Night and day are given over to pleasure
And they think it will last a thousand autumns.

Unwearying autumns.
For them the yellow dogs howl portents in vain,
And what are they compared to the lady Riokushu,
  That was cause of hate!
Who among them is a man like Han-rei
      Who departed alone with his mistress,
With her hair unbound, and he his own skiffs-man!

  By Rihaku.

Lament of the Frontier Guard

By the North Gate, the wind blows full of sand,
Lonely from the beginning of time until now!
Trees fall, the grass goes yellow with autumn,
I climb the towers and towers
            to watch out the barbarous land:
Desolate castle, the sky, the wide desert.
There is no wall left to this village.
Bones white with a thousand frosts,
High heaps, covered with trees and grass;
Who brought this to pass?
Who was brought the flaming imperial anger?
Who has brought the army with drums and with kettle-drums?
Barbarous kings.
A gracious spring, turned to blood-ravenous autumn,
A turmoil of wars-men, spread over the middle kingdom,
Three hundred and sixty thousand,
And sorrow, sorrow like rain.
Sorrow to go, and sorrow, sorrow returning.
Desolate, desolate fields,
And no children of warfare upon them,
            No longer the men for offence and defence.
Ah, how shall you know the dreary sorrow at the North Gate,
With Rihoku's name forgotten,
And we guardsmen fed to the tigers.

                                              By Rihaku.

Exile's Letter

To So-Kin of Rakuyo, ancient friend, Chancellor of Gen.

Now I remember that you built me a special tavern
By the south side of the bridge at Ten-Shin.
With yellow gold and white jewels, we paid for the songs and
   laughter
And we were drunk for month after month, forgetting the kings and
   princes.
Intelligent men came drifting in, from the sea from the west border
And with them, and with you especially,
There was nothing at cross purpose,
And they made nothing of sea-crossing or of mountain-crossing,
If only they could be of that fellowship,
And we all spoke out our hearts and minds, and without regret.

And then I was sent off to South Wei,
                smothered in laurel groves,
And you to the north of Raku-hoku,
Till we had nothing but thoughts and memories in common.

And then, when separation had come to its worst
We met, and travelled into Sen-Go
Through all the thirty-six folds of the turning and twisting waters,
Into a valley of a thousand bright flowers,
That was the first valley;
And on into ten thousand valleys full of voices and pine-winds.

And with silver harness and reins of gold,
                prostrating themselves on the ground,
Out came the East of Kan foreman and his company.
And there came also the 'True-man' of Shi-yo to meet me,
Playing on a jewelled mouth-organ.
In the storied houses of San-Ko they gave us more Sennin music,
Many instruments, like the sound of young phoenix broods.
The foreman of Kan-Chu, drunk, danced
                because his long sleeves wouldn't keep still
With that music playing.
And I, wrapped in brocade, went to sleep with my head on his lap,
And my spirit so high it was all over the heavens.
And before the end of the day we were scattered like stars or rain.
I had to be off to So, far away over the waters,
You back to your river-bridge.
And your father, who was brave as a leopard,
Was governor in Hei-Shu and put down the barbarian rabble.
And one May he had you send for me,
                despite the long distance;
And what with broken wheels and so on, I won't say it wasn't hard
    going,
Over roads twisted like sheep's guts.
And I was still going, late in the year,
                in the cutting wind from the North,
And thinking how little you cared for the cost,
                and you caring enough to pay it.
Then what a reception:
Red jade cups, food well set on a blue jeweled table,
And I was drunk, and had no thought of returning.
And you would walk out with me to the western corner of the castle,
To the dynastic temple, with water about it clear as blue jade,
With boats floating, and the sound of mouth-organs and drums,
With ripples like dragon-scales, going glass green on the water,
Pleasure lasting, with courtesans going and coming without
    hindrance,
With the willow-flakes falling like snow,

88

And the vermilioned girls getting drunk about sunset,
And the waters a hundred feet deep reflecting green eyebrows
—Eyebrows painted green are a fine sight in young moonlight,
Gracefully painted—
And the girls singing back at each other,
Dancing in transparent brocade,
And the wind lifting the song, and interrupting it,
Tossing it up under the clouds.
    And all this comes to an end.
    And is not again to be met with.
I went up to the court for examination,
Tried Layu's luck, offered the Choyo song,
And got no promotion,
    and went back to the East Mountains white-headed.
And once again, later, we met at the South bridge-head.
And then the crowd broke up, you went north to San palace,
And if you ask how I regret that parting:
  It is like the flowers falling at Spring's end,
    Confused, whirled in a tangle.
What is the use of talking, and there is no end of talking,
There is no end of things in the heart.

I call in the boy,
Have him sit on his knees here
    To seal this,
And send it a thousand miles, thinking.

           By Rihaku.

Four Poems of Departure

From Rihaku

Light rain is on the light dust.
The willows of the inn-yard
Will be going greener and greener,
But you, Sir, had better take wine ere your departure,
For you will have no friends about you
When you come to the gates of Go.

Separation on the River Kiang

Ko-jin goes west from Ko-kaku-ro,
The smoke flowers are blurred over the river.
His lone sail blots the far sky.
And now I see only the river,
   The long Kiang, reaching heaven.

Taking Leave of a Friend

Blue mountains to the north of the walls,
White river winding about them;
Here we must make separation
And go out through a thousand miles of dead grass.

Mind like a floating white cloud,
Sunset like the parting of old acquaintances
Who bow over their clasped hands at a distance.
Our horses neigh to each other
        as we are departing

Leave-taking Near Shoku

They say the roads of Sanso are steep,
Sheer as the mountains.
The walls rise in a man's face,
Clouds grow out of the hill
        at his horse's bridle.
Sweet trees are on the paved way of the Shin,
Their trunks burst through the paving,
And freshets are bursting their ice
        in the midst of Shoku, a proud city.

Men's fates are already set,
There is no need of asking diviners.

The City of Choan

The phoenix are at play on their terrace.
The phoenix are gone, the river flows on alone.
Flowers and grass
Cover over the dark path
         where lay the dynastic house of the Go.
The bright cloths and bright caps of the Shin
Are now the base of old hills.

The Three Mountains fall through the far heaven,
The isle of White Heron
         splits the two streams apart.
Now the high clouds cover the sun
And I can not see Choan afar
And I am sad.

South-Folk in Cold Country

The Dai horse neighs against the bleak wind of Etsu,.
The birds of Etsu have no love for En, in the north,
Emotion is born out of habit,[1]
Yesterday we went out of the Wild-Goose gate,
Today from the Dragon-Pen.
Surprised. Desert turmoil. Sea sun.
Flying snow bewilders the barbarian heaven.
Lice swarm like ants over our accoutrements.
Mind and spirit drive on the feathery banners.
Hard fight gets no reward.
Loyalty is hard to explain.
Who will be sorry for General Rishogu,
            the swift moving,
Whose white head is lost for this province?

---

1. I.e., we have been warring from one end of the empire to the other, now east,
now west, on each border.

93

From *Lustra*

And the days are not full enough

And the days are not full enough
And the nights are not full enough
And life slips by like a field mouse
Not shaking the grass

The Garret

Come, let us pity those who are better off than we are.
Come, my friend, and remember
          that the rich have butlers and no friends,
And we have friends and no butlers.
Come, let us pity the married and the unmarried.

Dawn enters with little feet
          like a gilded Pavlova
And I am near my desire.
Nor has life in it aught better
Than this hour of clear coolness
          the hour of waking together.

The Garden

En robe de parade.
    Samain

Like a skein of loose silk blown against a wall
She walks by the railing of a path in Kensington Gardens,
And she is dying piece-meal
    of a sort of emotional anaemia.

And round about there is a rabble
Of the filthy, sturdy, unkillable infants of the very poor.
They shall inherit the earth.

In her is the end of breeding.
Her boredom is exquisite and excessive.
She would like some one to speak to her,
And is almost afraid that I
    will commit that indiscretion.

Salutation

O generation of the thoroughly smug
        and thoroughly uncomfortable,
I have seen fishermen picnicking in the sun,
I have seen them with untidy families,
I have seen their smiles full of teeth
        and heard ungainly laughter.
And I am happier than you are,
And they were happier than I am;
And the fish swim in the lake
        and do not even own clothing.

Commission

Go, my songs, to the lonely and the unsatisfied,
Go also to the nerve-wracked, go to the enslaved-by-convention,
Bear to them my contempt for their oppressors.
Go as a great wave of cool water,
Bear my contempt of oppressors.

Speak against unconscious oppression,
Speak against the tyranny of the unimaginative,
Speak against bonds.
Go to the bourgeoise who is dying of her ennuis,
Go to the women in suburbs.
Go to the hideously wedded,
Go to them whose failure is concealed,
Go to the unluckily mated,
Go to the bought wife,
Go to the woman entailed.

Go to those who have delicate lust,
Go to those whose delicate desires are thwarted,
Go like a blight upon the dulness of the world;
Go with your edge against this,
Strengthen the subtle cords,
Bring confidence upon the algae and the tentacles of the soul.

Go in a friendly manner,
Go with an open speech.
Be eager to find new evils and new good,

Be against all forms of oppression.
Go to those who are thickened with middle age,
To those who have lost their interest.

Go to the adolescent who are smothered in family—
Oh how hideous it is
To see three generations of one house gathered together!
It is like an old tree with shoots,
And with some branches rotted and falling.

Go out and defy opinion,
Go against this vegetable bondage of the blood.
Be against all sorts of mortmain.

A Pact

I make a pact with you, Walt Whitman—
I have detested you long enough.
I come to you as a grown child
Who has had a pig-headed father;
I am old enough now to make friends.
It was you that broke the new wood,
Now is a time for carving.
We have one sap and one root—
Let there be commerce between us.

Dance Figure

For the Marriage in Cana of Galilee

Dark-eyed,
O woman of my dreams,
Ivory sandalled,
There is none like thee among the dancers,
None with swift feet.

I have not found thee in the tents,
In the broken darkness.
I have not found thee at the well-head
Among the women with pitchers.

Thine arms are as a young sapling under the bark;
Thy face as a river with lights.

White as an almond are thy shoulders;
As new almonds stripped from the husk.

They guard thee not with eunuchs;
Not with bars of copper.

Gilt turquoise and silver are in the place of thy rest.
A brown robe, with threads of gold woven in patterns,
        hast thou gathered about thee,
O Nathat-Ikanaie, "Tree-at-the-river."

As a rillet among the sedge are thy hands upon me;
Thy fingers a frosted stream.

Thy maidens are white like pebbles;
Their music about thee!

There is none like thee among the dancers;
None with swift feet.

The Rest

O helpless few in my country,
O remnant enslaved!

Artists broken against her,
A-stray, lost in the villages,
Mistrusted, spoken-against,

Lovers of beauty, starved
Thwarted with systems,
Helpless against the control;

You who can not wear yourselves out
By persisting to successes,
You who can only speak,
Who can not steel yourselves into reiteration;

You of the finer sense,
Broken against false knowledge,
You who can know at first hand,
Hated, shut in, mistrusted:

Take thought;
I have weathered the storm,
I have beaten out my exile.

Further Instructions

Come, my songs, let us express our baser passions.
Let us express our envy for the man with a steady job and no worry
    about the future.
You are very idle, my songs,
I fear you will come to a bad end.
You stand about the streets,
You loiter at the corners and bus-stops,
You do next to nothing at all.

You do not even express our inner nobilities,
You will come to a very bad end.

And I? I have gone half-cracked.
I have talked to you so much that
                    I almost see you about me,
Insolent little beasts! Shameless! Devoid of clothing!

But you, newest song of the lot,
You are not old enough to have done much mischief.
I will get you a green coat out of China
With dragons worked upon it.
I will get you the scarlet silk trousers
From the statue of the infant Christ at Santa Maria Novella;
Lest they say we are lacking in taste,
Or that there is no caste in this family.

A Song of the Degrees

I

Rest me with Chinese colours,
For I think the glass is evil.

II

The wind moves above the wheat—
With a silver crashing,
A thin war of metal.

I have known the golden disc,
I have seen it melting above me.
I have known the stone-bright place,
        The hall of clear colours.

III

O glass subtly evil, O confusion of colours!
O light bound and bent in, O soul of the captive,
Why am I warned? Why am I sent away?
Why is your glitter full of curious mistrust?
O glass subtle and cunning, O powdery gold!
O filaments of amber, two-faced iridescence!

Ité

Go, my songs, seek your praise from the young and from the
  intolerant,
Move among the lovers of perfection alone.
Seek ever to stand in the hard Sophoclean light
And take you wounds from it gladly.

The Bath Tub

As a bathtub lined with white porcelain,
When the hot water gives out or goes tepid,
So is the slow cooling of our chivalrous passion,
O my much praised but-not-altogether-satisfactory lady.

Meditatio

When I carefully consider the curious habits of dogs
I am compelled to conclude
That man is the superior animal.

When I consider the curious habits of man
I confess, my friend, I am puzzled.

The Seeing Eye

The small dogs look at the big dogs;
They observe unwieldy dimensions
And curious imperfections of odor.

Here is the formal male group:
The young men look upon their seniors,
They consider the elderly mind
And observe its inexplicable correlations.

Said Tsin-Tsu:
It is only in small dogs and the young
That we find minute observation.

Fan-Piece, For Her Imperial Lord

O fan of white silk,
    clear as frost on the grass-blade,
You also are laid aside.

Ts'ai Chi'h

The petals fall in the fountain,
     the orange-coloured rose-leaves,
Their ochre clings to the stone.

Alba

As cool as the pale wet leaves
                            of lily-of-the-valley
She lay beside me in the dawn.

In a Station of the Metro

The apparition of these faces in the crowd;
Petals on a wet, black bough.

The Encounter

All the while they were talking the new morality
Her eyes explored me.
And when I arose to go
Her fingers were like the tissue
Of a Japanese paper napkin.

"Ione, Dead the Long Year"

Empty are the ways,
Empty are the ways of this land
And the flowers
                Bend over with heavy heads.
They bend in vain.
Empty are the ways of this land
                Where Ione
Walked once, and now does not walk
But seems like a person just gone.

Tame Cat

"It rests me to be among beautiful women
Why should one always lie about such matters?

I repeat:
It rests me to converse with beautiful women
Even though we talk nothing but nonsense,

The purring of the invisible antennae
Is both stimulating and delightful."

L'Art, 1910

Green arsenic smeared on an egg-white cloth,
Crushed strawberries! Come, let us feast our eyes.

Epilogue

O chansons foregoing
You were a seven days' wonder.
When you came out in the magazines
You created considerable stir in Chicago,
And now you are stale and worn out,
You're a very depleted fashion,
A hoop-skirt, a calash,
An homely, transient antiquity.

Only emotion remains.

Your emotions?
              Are those of a maître-de-café.

The Lake Isle

O God, O Venus, O Mercury, patron of thieves,
Give me in due time, I beseech you, a little tobacco-shop,
With the little bright boxes
            piled up neatly upon the shelves
And the loose fragment cavendish
            and the shag,
And the bright Virginia
            loose under the bright glass cases,
And a pair of scales not too greasy,
And the votailles dropping in for a word or two in passing,
For a flip word, and to tidy their hair a bit.

O God, O Venus, O Mercury, patron of thieves,
Lend me a little tobacco-shop,
            or install me in any profession
Save this damn'd profession of writing,
            where one needs one's brains all the time.

Ancient Wisdom, Rather Cosmic

So-shu dreamed,
And having dreamed that he was a bird, a bee, and a butterfly,
He was uncertain why he should try to feel like anything else,

Hence his contentment.

The Game of Chess

Dogmatic Statement Concerning the Game of Chess:
Theme for a Series of Pictures

Red knights, brown bishops, bright queens,
Striking the board, falling in strong "L"s of colour.
Reaching and striking in angles,
            holding lines in one colour.
This board is alive with light;
            these pieces are living in form,
Their moves break and reform the pattern:
            Luminous green from the rooks,
Clashing with "X"s of queens,
            looped with the knight-leaps.

"Y" pawns, cleaving, embanking!
Whirl! Centripetal! Mate! King down in the vortex,
Clash, leaping of bands, straight strips of hard colour,
Blocked lights working in. Escapes. Renewal of contest.

Sennin Poem by Kakuhaku

The red and green kingfishers
        flash between the orchids and clover,
One bird casts its gleam on another.

Green vines hang through the high forest,
They weave a whole roof to the mountain,
The lone man sits with shut speech,
He purrs and pats the clear strings.
He throws his heart up through the sky,
He bites through the flower pistil
        and brings up a fine fountain.
The red-pine-tree god looks at him and wonders.
He rides through the purple smoke to visit the sennin,
He takes "Floating Hill"[1] by the sleeve,
He claps his hand on the back of the great white sennin.

But you, you dam'd crowd of gnats,
Can you even tell the age of a turtle?

---

1. Name of a sennin, or spirit.

A Ballad of the Mulberry Road

The sun rises in south east corner of things
To look on the tall house of the Shin
For they have a daughter named Rafu,
    (pretty girl)
She made the name for herself: "Gauze Veil,"
For she feeds mulberries to silkworms.
    She gets them by the south wall of the town.
With green strings she makes the warp of her basket
She makes the shoulder-straps of her basket
    from the boughs of Ketsura,
And she piles her hair up on the left side of her head-piece.

Her earring are made of pearl,
Her underskirt is of green pattern-silk,
Her overskirt is the same silk dyed in purple,
And when men going by look at Rafu
    They set down their burdens,
They stand and twirl their moustaches.

(Fenollosa Mss., very early)

Old Idea of Choan by Rosoriu

I

The narrow streets cut into the wide highway at Choan,
Dark oxen, white horses,
        drag on the seven coaches with outriders
The coaches are perfumed wood,
The jewelled chair is held up at the crossway,
Before the royal lodge:
        a glitter of golden saddles, awaiting the princess;
They eddy before the gate of the barons.
The canopy embroidered with dragons
        drinks in and casts back the sun.

Evening comes.
        The trappings are bordered with mist.
The hundred cords of mist are spread through
        and double the trees,
Night birds, and night women,
        spread out their sounds through the gardens.

II

Birds with flowery wing, hovering butterflies
        crowd over the thousand gates,
Trees that glitter like jade,
        terraces tinged with silver,

The seed of a myriad hues,
A net-work of arbors and passages and covered ways,
Double towers, winged roofs,
          border the net-work of ways:
A place of felicitous meeting.
Riu's house stands out on the sky,
          with glitter of color
As Butei of Kan made the high golden lotus
          to gather his dews,
Before it another house which I do not know:
How shall we know all the friends
          whom we meet on strange roadways?

To-Em-Mei's "The Unmoving Cloud"

"Wet springtime." says To-Em-Mei. "Wet spring in the garden."

I

The clouds have gathered, and gathered,
      and the rain falls and falls,
The eight ply of the heavens
      are all folded into one darkness,
And the wide, flat road stretches out.
I stop in my room towards the East, quiet, quiet,
I pat my new cask of wine.
My friends are estranged, or far distant,
I bow my head and stand still.

II

Rain, rain, and the clouds have gathered,
The eight ply of the heavens are darkness,
The flat land is turned into river.
      "Wine, wine, here is wine!"
I drink by my eastern window.
I think of talking and man,
And no boat, no carriage, approaches.

III

The trees in my east-looking garden
        are bursting out with new twigs,
They try to stir new affection

And men say the sun and moon keep on moving
        because they can't find a soft seat.

The birds flutter to rest in my tree,
        and I think I have heard them saying,
"It is not that there are no other men
But we like this fellow the best,
But however we long to speak
He can not know of our sorrow."

T'ao Yuan Ming
A.D.365–427

Villanelle: The Psychological Hour

I

I had over-prepared the event,
          that much was ominous.
With middle-ageing care
          I had laid out just the right books.
I had almost turned down the pages.

          Beauty is so rare a thing.
          So few drink of my fountain.

So much barren regret,
So many hours wasted!
And now I watch, from the window,
          the rain, the wandering busses.

"Their little cosmos is shaken"—
          the air is alive with that fact.
In their parts of the city
          they are played on by diverse forces.
How do I know?
          Oh, I know well enough.
For them there is something afoot.
          As for me;
I had over-prepared the event—

          Beauty is so rare a thing.

So few drink of my fountain.

Two friends: a breath of the forest . . .
Friends? Are people less friends
        because one has just, at last, found them?
Twice they promised to come.
                "Between the night and the morning?"

Beauty would drink of my mind.
Youth would awhile forget
        my youth is gone from me.

II

(Speak up! You have danced so stiffly?
        Someone admired your works,
        And said so frankly.

        "Did you talk like a fool,
        The first night?
        The second evening?"

"*But* they promised again:
                'To-morrow at tea-time.'")

III

Now the third day is here—
        no word from either;
No word from her nor him,
Only another man's note:
                "Dear Pound, I am leaving England."

Homage to Quintus Septimius Florentis Christianus

(Ex libris Graeca)

I

Theodorus will be pleased at my death,
And someone else will be pleased at the death of Theodorus,
And yet everyone speaks evil of death.

II

The place is Cyprian's, for she has ever the fancy
To be looking out across the bright sea,
Therefore the sailors are cheered, and the waves
Keep small with reverence, beholding her image.

Anyte

III

A sad and great evil is the expectation of death—
And there are also the inane expenses of the funeral;
Let us therefore cease from pitying the dead,
For after death there comes no other calamity.

Palladas

IV

Troy

Whither, O city, are your profits and your gilded shrines,
And your barbecues of great oxen,
And the tall women walking your streets, in gilt clothes,
With their perfumes in little alabaster boxes?
Where is the work of your home-born sculptors?

Time's tooth is into the lot, and war's and fate's too.
Envy has taken your all,
Save your douth and your story.

Agathas Scholasticus

V

Woman? Oh, woman is a consummate rage,
        but dead, or asleep, she pleases.
Take her. She has two excellent seasons.

Palladas

VI

Nicharcus upon Phidon his doctor

Phidon neither purged me nor touched me,
But I remembered the name of his fever medicine and died.

Impressions of François-Marie Arouet (de Voltaire)

I

Phyllidula and the Spoils of Gouvernet

Where, Lady, are the days
When you could go out in a hired hansom
Without footmen and equipments?
And dine in a soggy, cheap restaurant?
Phyllidula now, with your powdered Swiss footman
Clanking the door shut,
           and lying;
And carpets from Savonnier, and from Persia,
And your new service at dinner,
And plates from Germain,
And cabinets and chests from Martin (almost lacquer),
And your white vases from Japan,
And the lustre of diamonds,
Etcetera, etcetera, and etcetera?

II

To Madame du Châtelet

If you'd have me go on loving you
Give me back the time of the thing.

Will you give me dawn light at evening?
Time has driven me out of the fine plaisaunces,
The parks with the swards all over dew,
The grass going glassy with the light on it,
The green stretches where love is and the grapes
Hang in yellow-white and dark clusters ready for pressing.

And if now we can't fit with our time of life
There is not much but its evil left us.

Life gives us two minutes, two seasons—
          One to be dull in;
Two deaths—and to stop loving and being lovable,
That is the real death,
The other is little beside it.

Crying after the follies gone by me,
Quiet talking is all that is left us—
Gentle talking, not like the first talking, less lively;
And to follow after friendship, as they call it,
Weeping that we can follow naught else.

III

To Madame Lullin

You'll wonder that an old man of eighty
Can go on writing you verses. . . .

Grass showing under the snow,
Birds singing late in the year!

And Tibullus could say of his death, in his Latin:
"Delia, I would look on you, dying."

And Delia herself fading out,
Forgetting even her beauty.

From *Quia Pauper Amavi*

Moeurs Contemporaines

I

Mr. Styrax

1   Mr. Hecatomb Styrax, the owner of a large estate
                and of large muscles,
A "blue" and a climber of mountains, has married
                at the age of 28,
He being at that age a virgin,
The term "virgo" being made male in mediaeval latinity;
    His ineptitudes
Having driven his wife from one religious excess to another.
She has abandoned the vicar
For he was lacking in vehemence;
She is now the high-priestess
Of a modern and ethical cult,
        And even now, Mr. Styrax
        Does not believe in aesthetics.

2   His brother has taken to gipsies,
But the son-in-law of Mr. H. Styrax
Objects to perfumed cigarettes.
        In the parlance of Niccolo Machiavelli:
        "Thus things proceed in their circle";
        And thus the empire is maintained.

II

Clara

At sixteen she was a potential celebrity
With a distaste for caresses.
She now writes to me from a convent;
Her life is obscure and troubled;
Her second husband will not divorce her;
Her mind is, as ever, uncultivated,
And no issue presents itself.
She does not desire her children,
Or any more children.
Her ambition is vague and indefinite,
She will neither stay in, nor come out.

III

Soiree

Upon learning that the mother wrote verses,
And that the father wrote verses,
And that the youngest son was in a publisher's office,
And that the friend of the second daughter
was undergoing a novel,
The young American pilgrim
Exclaimed:
        "This is a darn'd clever bunch!"

IV

Sketch 48 b. 11

At the age of 27
Its home mail is still opened by its maternal parent

And its office mail may be opened by
                              its parent of the opposite gender.
It is an officer,
              and a gentleman,
                              and an architect.

V

"Nodier raconte . . ."

1   At a friend of my wife's there is a photograph,
A faded, pale brownish photograph,
Of the times when the sleeves were large,
Silk, stiff and large above the *lacertus*,
That is, the upper arm,
And décolleté. . . .
                              It is a lady,
She sits at a harp,
Playing,

And by her left foot, in a basket,
Is an infant, aged about 14 months,
The infant beams at the parent,
The parent re-beams at its offspring.
The basket is lined with satin,
There is a satin-like bow on the harp.

2   And in the home of the novelist
There is a satin-like bow on an harp.

You enter and pass hall after hall
And conservatory follows conservatory,
Lilies lift their white symbolical cups,
Whence their symbolical pollen has been excerpted,
Near them I noticed an harp

And the blue satin ribbon,
And the copy of "Hatha Yoga"
And the neat piles of unopened, unopening books,

And she spoke to me of the monarch,
And of the purity of her soul.

VI

Stele

After years of continence
  he hurled himself in a sea of six women.
Now, quenched as the brand of Meleagar,
  he lies by the poluphloisboious sea-coast.

Παρὰ θῖνα Πολνφλοίς βοιο θαλàσσης

SISTE VIATOR.

VII

I Vecchii

They will come no more,
The old men with beautiful manners.

Il était comme un tout petit garçon
With his blouse full of apples
And sticking out all the way round;
Blagueur! "Con gli occhi onesti e tardi,"

And he said:
  "Oh! Abelard!" as if the topic

Were much too abstruse for his comprehension,
And he talked about "the Great Mary,"
And said: "Mr. Pound is shocked at my levity."
When it turned out he meant Mrs. Ward.

And the other was rather like my bust by Gaudier,
Or like a real Texas colonel,
He said: "Why flay dead horses?
"There was once a man called Voltaire."

And he said they used to cheer Verdi.
In Rome, after the opera,
And the guards couldn't stop them,

And that was an anagram for Vittorio
Emanuele Re D' Italia,
And the guards couldn't stop them.

      Old men with beautiful manners,
Sitting in the Row of a morning,
Walking on the Chelsea Embankment.

VIII

Ritratto

And she said:
        "You remember Mr. Lowell,
"He was your ambassador here?"
And I said: "That was before I arrived."
And she said:
        "He stomped into my bedroom. . . .
(By that time she had got on to Browning.)
" . . . stomped into my bedroom. . . .
"And said: 'Do I,
"'I ask you, Do I

"'Care too much for society dinners?'
"And I wouldn't say that he didn't.
"Shelley used to live in this house."

She was a very old lady,
I never saw her again.

From Homage to Sextus Propertius

I

Shades of Callimachus, Coan ghosts of Philetas
It is in your grove I would walk,
I who come first from the clear font
Bringing the Grecian orgies into Italy,
                      and the dance into Italy.
Who hath taught you so subtle a measure,
                    in what hall have you heard it;
What foot beat out your time-bar,
                  what water has mellowed your whistles?

Out-weariers of Apollo will, as we know, continue their Martian
    generalities,
                We have kept our erasers in order,
A new-fangled chariot follows the flower-hung horses;
A young Muse with young loves clustered about her
                  ascends with me into the æther, . . .
And there is no high-road to the Muses.

Annalists will continue to record Roman reputations,
Celebrities from the Trans-Caucasus will belaud Roman celebrities
And expound the distentions of Empire,

But for something to read in normal circumstances?
For a few pages brought down from the forked hill unsullied?
             I ask a wreath which will not crush my head.

                    And there is no hurry about it;
I shall have, doubtless, a boom after my funeral,
Seeing that long standing increases all things
                              regardless of quality. . . .

III

Midnight, and a letter comes to me from our mistress:
                    Telling me to come to Tibur, *At* once!!:
Bright tips reach up from twin towers,
        Anienan spring water falls into flat-spread pools.

What is to be done about it?
                Shall I entrust myself to entangled shadows,
Where bold hands may do violence to my person?
Yet if I postpone my obedience
                        because of this respectable terror
I shall be prey to lamentations worse than a nocturnal assailant.
And I shall be in the wrong,
                        and it will last a twelve month,
For her hands have no kindness me-ward,

Nor is there anyone to whom lovers are not sacred at midnight
And in the Via Sciro.

If any man would be a lover
                        he may walk on the Scythian coast,
No barbarism would go to the extent of doing him harm,
The moon will carry his candle,
                        the stars will point out the stumbles,
Cupid will carry lighted torches before him
                        and keep mad dogs off his ankles.
Thus all roads are perfectly safe
                        and at any hour;
Who so indecorous as to shed the pure gore of a suitor?!

Cypris is his cicerone.
What if undertakers follow my track,
                          such a death is worth dying.
She would bring frankincense and wreaths to my tomb,
          She would sit like an ornament on my pyre.

Gods' aid, let not my bones lie in a public location
          with crowds too assiduous in their crossing of it;
For thus are tombs of lovers most desecrated.

May a woody and sequestered place cover me with its foliage
Or may I inter beneath the hummock
                          of some as yet uncatalogued sand;
At any rate I shall not have my epitaph in a high road.

IV

Difference of Opinion with Lygdamus

Tell me the truths which you hear of our constant young lady,
          Lygdamus,
And may the bought yoke of a mistress lie with
                          equitable weight on your shoulders;
For I am swelled up with inane pleasurabilities
                          and deceived by your reference
          To things which you think I would like to believe.

No messenger should come wholly empty,
                          and a slave should fear plausibilities;
     Much conversation is as good as having a home.
     Out with it, tell it to me, all of it, from the beginning,
I guzzle with outstretched ears.
Thus? She wept into uncombed hair,
                          And you saw it.
Vast waters flowed from her eyes?

                              You, you Lygdamus
Saw her stretched on her bed,—
                    it was no glimpse in a mirror;
No gawds on her snowy hands, no orfevrerie,
Sad garment draped on her slender arms.
Her escritoires lay shut by the bed-feet.
Sadness hung over the house, and the desolated female attendants
Were desolated because she had told them her dreams.

She was veiled in the midst of that place,
Damp woolly hankerchiefs were stuffed into her undryable eyes,
And a querulous noise responded to our solicitous reprobations.

        For which things you will get a reward from me,
                              Lygdamus?
To say many things is equal to having a home.
And the other woman "has not enticed me
                         by her pretty manners,
"She has caught me with herbaceous poison,
                    she twiddles the spiked wheel of a rhombus,
"She stews puffed frogs, snake's bones, the moulded feathers of
    screech owls,

"She binds me with ravvles of shrouds.
                    "Black spiders spin in her bed!
"Let her lovers snore at her in the morning!
                    "May the gout cramp up her feet!
        "Does he like me to sleep here alone, Lydgamus?
        "Will he say nasty things at my funeral?"

And you expect me to believe this
                    after twelve months of discomfort?

From *Hugh Selwyn Mauberley*

From H. S. Mauberley
(Life and Contacts)

E.P.

Ode pour l'élection de son sépulchre

For three years, out of key with his time,
He strove to resuscitate the dead art
Of poetry; to maintain "the sublime"
In the old sense. Wrong from the start—

No, hardly, but, seeing he had been born
In a half savage country, out of date;
Bent resolutely on wringing lilies from the acorn;
Capaneus; trout for factitious bait;

Ἴδμεν γύρ τοι πάνθ᾽, ὅς᾽ἐνὶ Τροίη
Caught in the unstopped ear;
Giving the rocks small lee-way
The chopped seas held him, therefore, that year.

His true Penelope was Flaubert,
He fished by obstinate isles;
Observed the elegance of Circe's hair
Rather than the mottoes on sun-dials.

Unaffected by "the march of events,"
He passed from men's memory in *l'an trentiesme*
De son eage; the case presents
No adjunct to the Muses' diadem.

II

The age demanded an image
Of its accelerated grimace,
Something for the modern stage,
Not, at any rate, an Attic grace;

Not, not certainly, the obscure reveries
Of the inward gaze;
Better mendacities
Than the classics in paraphrase!

The "age demanded" chiefly a mould in plaster,
Made with no loss of time,
A prose kinema, not, not assuredly, alabaster
Or the "sculpture" of rhyme. . . .

IV

These fought, in any case,
and some believing, pro domo, in any case . .

Some quick to arm,
some for adventure,
some from fear of weakness,
some from fear of censure,
some for love of slaughter, in imagination,
learning later . . .

some in fear, learning love of slaughter;
Died some pro patria, non dulce non et decor . .

walked eye-deep in hell
believing in old men's lies, then unbelieving
came home, home to a lie,
home to many deceits,
home to old lies and new infamy;

usury age-old and age-thick
and liars in public places.

Daring as never before, wastage as never before.
Young blood and high blood,
Fair cheeks, and fine bodies;

fortitude as never before

frankness as never before,
disillusions as never told in the old days,
hysterias, trench confessions,
laughter out of dead bellies.

V

There died a myriad,
And of the best, among them,
For an old bitch gone in the teeth,
For a botched civilization.

Charm, smiling at the good mouth,
Quick eyes gone under earth's lid,

For two gross of broken statues,
For a few thousand battered books.

Yeux Glauques

Gladstone was still respected,
When John Ruskin produced
"Kings Treasuries"; Swinburne
And Rossetti still abused.

Fœtid Buchanan lifted up his voice
When that faun's head of hers
Became a pastime for
Painters and adulterers.

The Burne-Jones cartons
Have preserved her eyes;
Still, at the Tate, they teach
Cophetua to rhapsodize;

Thin like brook-water,
With a vacant gaze.
The English Rubaiyat was still-born
In those days.

The thin, clear gaze, the same
Still darts out faun-like from the half-ruin'd face,
Questing and passive. . . .
"Ah, poor Jenny's case" . . .

Bewildered that a world
Shows no surprise
At her last maquero's
Adulteries.

"Siena Mi Fe,' Disfecemi Maremma"

Among the pickled fœtuses and bottled bones,
Engaged in perfecting the catalogue,

I found the last scion of the
Senatorial families of Strasbourg, Monsieur Verog.

For two hours he talked of Gallifet;
Of Dowson; of the Rhymers' Club;
Told me how Johnson (Lionel) died
By falling from a high stool in a pub . . .

But showed no trace of alcohol
At the autopsy, privately performed—
Tissue preserved—the pure mind
Arose toward Newman as the whiskey warmed.

Dowson found harlots cheaper than hotels;
Headlam for uplift; Image impartially imbued
With raptures for Bacchus, Terpsichore and the Church.
So spoke the author of "The Dorian Mood,"

M. Verog, out of step with the decade,
Detached from his contemporaries,
Neglected by the young,
Because of these reveries.

Brennbaum

The sky-like limpid eyes,
The circular infant's face,
The stiffness from spats to collar
Never relaxing into grace;

The heavy memories of Horeb, Sinai and the forty years,
Showed only when the daylight fell
Level across the face
Of Brennbaum "The Impeccable."

Mr. Nixon

In the cream gilded cabin of his steam yacht
Mr. Nixon advised me kindly, to advance with fewer
Dangers of delay. "Consider
     "Carefully the reviewer.

"I was as poor as you are;
"When I began I got, of course,
"Advance on royalties, fifty at first," said Mr. Nixon,
"Follow me, and take a column,
"Even if you have to work free.

"Butter reviewers. From fifty to three hundred
"I rose in eighteen months;
"The hardest nut I had to crack
"Was Dr. Dundas.

"I never mentioned a man but with the view
"Of selling my own works.
"The tip's a good one, as for literature
"It gives no man a sinecure."

And no one knows, at sight a masterpiece.
And give up verse, my boy,
There's nothing in it.

* * *

Likewise a friend of Bloughram's once advised me:
Don't kick against the pricks,
Accept opinion. The "Nineties" tried your game
And died, there's nothing in it.

X

Beneath the sagging roof
The stylist has taken shelter,
Unpaid, uncelebrated,
At last from the world's welter

Nature receives him,
With a placid and uneducated mistress
He exercises his talents
And the soil meets his distress.

The haven from sophistications and contentions
Leaks through its thatch;
He offers succulent cooking;
The door has a creaking latch.

XI

"Conservatrix of Milésien"
Habits of mind and feeling,
Possibly. But in Ealing
With the most bank-clerkly of Englishmen?

No, "Milésian" is an exaggeration.
No instinct has survived in her
Older than those her grandmother
Told her would fit her station.

XII

"Daphne with her thighs in bark
Stretches toward me her leafy hands,"—
Subjectively. In the stuffed-satin drawing-room
I await The Lady Valentine's commands,

Knowing my coat has never been
Of precisely the fashion
To stimulate, in her,
A durable passion;

Doubtful, somewhat, of the value
Of well-gowned approbation
Of literary effort,
But never of The Lady Valentine's vocation:

Poetry, her border of ideas,
The edge, uncertain, but a means of blending
With other strata
Where the lower and higher have ending;

A hook to catch the Lady Jane's attention,
A modulation toward the theatre,
Also, in the case of revolution,
A possible friend and comforter.

* * *

Conduct, on the other hand, the soul
"Which the highest cultures have nourished"
To Fleet St. where
Dr. Johnson flourished;

Beside this thoroughfare
The sale of half-hose has
Long since superseded the cultivation
Of Pierian roses.

Envoi (1919)

Go, dumb-born book,
Tell her that sang me once that song of Lawes;
Hadst thou but song
As thou hast subjects known,
Then were there cause in thee that should condone
Even my faults that heavy upon me lie
And build her glories their longevity.

Tell her that sheds
Such treasure in the air,
Recking naught else but that her graces give
Life to the moment,
I would bid them live
As roses might, in magic amber laid,
Red overwrought with orange and all made
One substance and one colour
Braving time.

Tell her that goes
With song upon her lips
But sings not out the song, nor knows
The maker of it, some other mouth,
May be as fair as hers,
Might, in new ages, gain her worshippers,
When our two dusts with Waller's shall be laid,
Siftings on siftings in oblivion,
Till change hath broken down
All things save Beauty alone.

Medallion

Luini in porcelain!
The grand piano
Utters a profane
Protest with her clear soprano.

The sleek head emerges
From the gold-yellow frock
As Anadyomene in the opening
Pages of Reinach.

Honey-red, closing the face-oval,
A basket-work of braids which seem as if they were
Spun in King Minos' hall
From metal, or intractable amber;

The face-oval beneath the glaze,
Bright in its suave bounding-line, as,
Beneath half-watt rays,
The eyes turn topaz.

From *Umbra*

Phanopoeia

I

Rose White, Yellow, Silver

The swirl of light follows me through the square,
The smoke of incense
Mounts from the four horns of my bed-posts,
The water-jet of gold light bears us up through the ceilings;
Lapped in the gold-coloured flame I descend through the aether.
The silver ball forms in my hand,
It falls and rolls to your feet.

II

SALTUS

The swirling sphere has opened
        and you are caught up to the skies,
You are englobed in my sapphire.
                                    Io! Io!

You have perceived the blades of the flame
The flutter of sharp-edged sandals.

The folding and lapping brightness
Has held in the air before you.

You have perceived the leaves of the flame.

III

Concava Vallis

The wire-like bands of colour involute mount from my fingers;
I have wrapped the wind round your shoulders
And the molten metal of your shoulders
    bends into turn of the wind,

AOI!
The whirling tissue of light
    is woven and grows solid beneath us;
The sea-clear sapphire of air, the sea-dark clarity,
    stretches both sea-cliff and ocean.

The Alchemist

Chant for the Transmutation of Metals

Saîl of Claustra, Aelis, Azalais,
As you move among the bright trees;
As your voices, under the larches of Paradise
Make a clear sound,
Saîl of Claustra, Aelis, Azalais,
Raimona, Tibors, Berangèrë,
'Neath the dark gleam of the sky;
Under night, the peacock-throated,
Bring the saffron-coloured shell,
Bring the red gold of the maple,
Bring the light of the birch tree in autumn
Mirals, Cembelins, Audiards,
                                        Remember this fire.

Elain, Tireis, Alcmena
'Mid the silver rustling of wheat,
Agradiva, Anhes, Ardenca,
From the plum-coloured lake, in stillness,
From the molten dyes of the water
Bring the burnished nature of fire;
Briseis, Lianor, Loica,
From the wide earth and the olive,
From the poplars weeping their amber,
By the bright flame of the fishing torch
                                        Remember this fire.

Midonz, with the gold of the sun, the leaf of the poplar, by the light
    of the amber,
Midonz, daughter of the sun, shaft of the tree, silver of the leaf, light
    of the yellow of the amber,
Midonz, gift of the God, gift of the light, gift of the amber of the sun,
                                Give light to the metal.
Anhes of Rocacoart, Ardenca, Aemelis,
From the power of grass,
From the white, alive in the seed,
From the heat of the bud,
From the copper of the leaf in autumn,
From the bronze of the maple, from the sap in the bough;
Lianor, Ioanna, Loica,
By the stir of the fin,
By the trout asleep in the grey green of water;
Vanna, Mandetta, Viera, Alodetta, Picarda, Manuela
From the red gleam of copper,
Ysaut, Ydone, slight rustling of leaves,
Vierna, Jocelynn, daring of spirits,
By the mirror of burnished copper,
            O Queen of Cypress,
Out of Erebus, the flat-lying breadth,
Breath that is stretched out beneath the world:
Out of Erebus, out of the flat waste of air, lying beneath the world;
Out of the brown leaf-brown colourless
            Bring the imperceptible cool.
Elain, Tireis, Alcmena,
            Quiet this metal!
Let the manes put off their terror, let them put off their aqueous
    bodies with fire.
Let them assume the milk-white bodies of agate.
Let them draw together the bones of the metal.

Selvaggia, Guiscarda, Mandetta,
            Rain flakes of gold on the water,
Azure and flaking silver of water,

Alcyon, Phaetona, Alcmena,
Pallor of silver, pale lustre of Latona,
By these, from the malevolence of the dew
                    Guard this alembic.
Elain, Tireis, Alodetta
            Quiet this metal.

Uncollected Poems

Ezra on the Strike

(First published in 1902)

Wal, Thanksgivin' do be comin' round.
With the price of turkeys on the bound,
And coal, by gum! Thet were just found,
    Is surely gettin' cheaper.

The winds will soon begin to howl,
And winter, in its yearly growl,
Across the medders begin to prowl,
    And Jack Frost gettin' deeper.

By shucks! It seems to me,
That you I orter be
Thankful, that our Ted could see
    A way to operate it.

I sez to Mandy, sure, sez I,
I'll bet thet air patch o' rye
Thet he'll squash 'em by-and-by,
    And he did, by cricket!

No use talkin', he's the man—
One of the best thet ever ran,
Fer didn't I turn Republican
    One o' the fust?

I 'lowed as how he'd beat the rest,
But old Si Perkins, he hemmed and guessed,
And sed as how it wuzn't best
     To meddle with the trust.

Now Pattison, he's gone up the flue,
And Coler, he kinder got there, tew,
So Si, put thet in your cud to chew,
     And give us all a rest.

Now thet I've had my little say
I wish you all a big Thanksgivin' day,
While I plod on to town with hay,
     And enjoy it best.

To the Raphaelite Latinists

(First published in 1908)

Ye fellowship that sing the woods and spring,
    Poets of joy that sing the day's delight,
    Poets of youth that 'neath the aisles of night
Your flowers and sighs against the lintels fling;

Who rose and myrtle in your garlands bring
    To marble altars, though their gods took flight
    Long ere your dream-shot eyes drank summer light
And wine of old time myth and vintaging,

Take of our praise one cup, though thin the wine
    That Bacchus may not bless nor Pan outpour:
Though reed pipe and the lyre be names upon
The wind, and moon-lit dreams be quite out-gone
    From ways we tread, one cup to names ye bore,
One wreath from ashes of your songs we twine!

The Fault of It

(First published in 1911)

Some may have blamed us that we cease to speak
Of things we spoke of in our verses early,
Saying: a lovely voice is such and such;
Saying: that lady's eyes were sad last week,
Wherein the world's whole joy is born and dies;
Saying: she hath this way or that, this much
Of grace, this way or that, this much
Of grace, this little misericorde;
Ask us no further word;
If we were proud, then proud to be so wise
Ask us no more of all the things ye heard;
We may not speak of them, they touch us nearly.

www.ingramcontent.com/pod-product-compliance
Lightning Source LLC
LaVergne TN
LVHW011157080426
835508LV00007B/461